King Lear

Illustrated by: Suman S. Roy
Compiled and Edited by: Tapasi De

Contents

1. King Lear at a Glance   3

2. Who's Who in the Play   4

3. King Lear   6

4. Post-reading Activities   41

5. About the Author   42

King Lear at a Glance

King Lear is one of the master works of Shakespeare in which Lear becomes the epitome of suffering and injustice. His two daughters abandon him and he banishes his youngest daughter who loved him the most. The play ends with several deaths and insanity of Lear leaving the readers full of fear and sympathy.

King Lear is known as one of the finest tragedies of Shakespeare. A *tragedy* is a play that is based on human suffering. It is a literary work in which the main character is destined to get ruined and hence he suffers extreme sorrow.

Who's Who in the Play

King Lear

King Lear is the central character of the play. He is childlike, passionate, cruel, kind, unlikable and sympathetic.

Cordelia

Cordelia is the youngest daughter of Lear and his favourite child also. Cordelia's chief characteristics are devotion, kindness, beauty and honesty.

Goneril and Regan

Goneril and Regan are the two elder daughters of King Lear. They are clever and know the art of flattery.

Edmund

He is the illegitimate son of Gloucester. He is bitter, bold and wicked.

Kent

The Earl of Kent is a nobleman and an unselfish, devoted supporter of King Lear. He is loyalty personified.

Edgar

Edgar, is the legitimate son of Gloucester. Edgar is dutiful and like Cordelia and suffers throughout the play.

Glossary
Illegitimate not sanctioned by law; unlawful

King Lear

Lear, the old King of Britain was worn out with age and the fatigues of government, being more than eighty years old. He was determined to take no further responsibility in the state affairs, but to leave the management of the kingdom to his children so that he might have time to prepare for his death, which was not far away. With this intention he called his three daughters to him, to know which of them loved him the most so that he could divide his kingdom according to the measurement of their affection. 'My dears, since I am growing old and will not live much longer, I wish to divide my kingdom amongst the three of you. But

Glossary
Intention a purpose, design or plan

before that, tell me how much each of you love me so that I may divide my kingdom on that basis.'

Now, King Lear had three daughters. The elder two were already married. Goneril, the eldest, declared that she loved her father more than words could tell. She said that he was dearer

to her than the light of her own eyes, dearer than her life and liberty. The king, delighted to hear from Goneril such assurance of her love, and thinking truly that her heart went with it, in a fit of fatherly fondness gave her and her husband one-third of his vast kingdom.

Then King Lear called his second daughter and asked her the same question. Regan, who was made of the same hollow metal as her elder sister, said, 'Father, you are the centre of all my affections! All other joys and pleasures seem dead in comparison to the joy of loving you.'

Lear blessed himself for having such loving children. He thought after all the handsome assurances which Regan his second daughter had made, he should bestow a third of his kingdom upon her and her husband, equal in size to that which he had already given away to Goneril, his eldest daughter.

Then turning to his youngest daughter, Cordelia, whom he called his 'joy', he asked what she had to say. He was sure that her loving speeches would be much stronger than her sisters', as she had always been his darling, and favoured by him above either of them. But Cordelia being disgusted with the flattery of her sisters, whose hearts she knew were far from their lips, made a rather curt reply; though she loved her father with all her heart. She well understood the intentions of her sisters which was to coax the old King out of his dominions, so that they and their husbands might reign in his lifetime. And so she said quietly, 'I love you father as much as is my duty as a daughter; not more, not less.'

The king, was shocked with such a speech of ingratitude from his favourite child. He said angrily, 'Cordelia, watch your words or you will be punished!'

But Cordelia was unperturbed. She said, 'Being my father you have given me good breeding and loved me. I have returned those duties back by obeying you, by loving you, and by honouring you. But I cannot frame such

Glossary
Ingratitude ungrateful, thankless
Unperturbed not concerned

pompous speeches as my sisters have done, or promise to love nothing else in the world other than you, father.'

She also said that why did her sisters have husbands if (as they said) they had no love for anything but their father? If she would ever get married, she was sure that her

husband would want half her love, half of her care and her duty. She also said that she would never marry like her sisters, if she had to love only her father!

The plainness of Cordelia's speech, which Lear called 'pride', enraged the old monarch very much. The rashness of his nature and old age had clouded his vision so much that he could not differentiate truth from flattery or words which came from the heart, from the words which were made for benefit. And so, in a fury of resentment he retracted the third part of his kingdom which he had reserved for Cordelia, gave it away, sharing it equally between her two sisters and their husbands, the Dukes of Albany and Cornwall. He did this in the presence of all his courtiers. He invested them jointly with all the power, revenue, and execution of government, only retaining to himself the name of king. He gave away all his royal powers except a hundred knights who were to be maintained for his service every month in each of his daughters' palaces in turns.

Glossary
Monarch king of a state
Retracted to draw back

All these incidents which were guided by so much anger and lack of reason that it filled all his courtiers with astonishment and sorrow; but none of them had the courage to interfere between this incensed king and his wrath.

There was but one person the Earl of Kent, who was beginning to speak a good word for Cordelia, when the passionate Lear commanded him to stop. But the good Kent was not to be discouraged. He had been ever loyal to Lear, whom he had honored as a King, loved as a father and followed as a master. And he had always considered that his life should be used against his royal master's enemies, not fearing to lose it when his master's safety was at stake. And now that Lear had become his own enemy, this faithful servant of the king opposed Lear to do good because Lear was behaving like a madman. He had been a most faithful counsellor of the king in the past, and that's why he implored him to realize that his youngest daughter loved him the most, and the empty words of his two elder daughters were hollow and meaningless.

Glossary
Wrath anger, fury
Counsellor a person who is trained to give advice on personal or psychological problems

The honest attempt of this good Earl of Kent to show what truth was only stirred up the king's wrath the more. He became like a frantic patient who kills his physician and loves his disease. Lear banished this true servant, and gave him but five days to make his preparations

Glossary
Physician a person qualified to give medical treatment
Banished send away someone from a country or a particular place as an official punishment

for departure. He also said that if on the sixth day this hated person was found within the realm of Britain, that moment he would be killed!

And so, Kent bade farewell to the king and left for the new country.

Before he went away, he said, 'I leave my dear Cordelia to the mercy of the Gods and the maid who was ever faithful to her and I will seek my fortunes in a new land.'

Then, the King of France and the Duke of Burgundy who were suitors of Cordelia were called in, to hear what King Lear had decided about her. They were called as the king wanted to know whether they would still continue in their courtship to Cordelia, now that she was under her father's displeasure and had no fortune of her own. The Duke of Burgundy at once declined the match, and would not take her as his wife upon such conditions. But the King of France, understanding the whole situation in which she had lost the love of her father said, 'I understand that the only fault of my dear Cordelia is the truthfulness of her tongue and

Glossary
Displeasure a feeling of disapproval

her incapability of flattery that has invited such a misfortune on her!' And then, taking the young Cordelia by the hand said that her virtues were a dowry above a kingdom. He asked Cordelia to take farewell of her sisters and of her father though he had been unkind, and leave for France to be his queen to reign over much more richer possessions than her sisters. And he called the Duke of Burgundy, in contempt, a 'waterish duke', because his love for this young maid had in a moment run all away like water.

Then Cordelia with weeping eyes took leave of her sisters, and asked them to love their father well and make good their professions. But her sisters were in no mood to listen to her.

They said, 'Sister, do not tell us our duty as we know it. Instead, spend time in pleasing your husband who thinks that you are his gift from his good fortune.'

Cordelia took all such sneers silently and said nothing. She departed with a heavy heart, for she knew the cunning nature of her sisters and

Glossary
Flattery praising falsely
Dowry an amount of property or money brought by a bride to her husband at the time of their marriage
Cunning crafty, shrewd

she wished her father in better hands as she was about to leave him in.

No sooner had Cordelia gone away that the devilish character of her sisters began to show themselves. Even before the passage of the first month, which Lear was to spend by agreement, with his daughter, Goneril, the old king began to find out the difference between promises and performances. This ungrateful daughter, having got from her father all that he had to bestow including his crown, began to grumble over the royal train which the old man had reserved for himself. She could not bear to see him and his knights. Every time Gonoril met her father she put on a frown and when the old man wanted to speak to her she would pretend to be sick or make an excuse not to speak to him. It was plain that she considered his old age a useless burden and his attendants an unnecessary expense. Not only she herself slackened in her expressions of duty to the king, but seeing her attitude towards the king, her very servants also began to ill-treat him. They would either refuse to obey his orders or contemptuously pretend not to hear them.

Lear could not help but notice this alteration in the behaviour of his daughter, but he shut

Glossary
Performance the act of performing something
Contemptuously to do something with contempt or scorn
Alteration the act of being altered

his eyes against it as long as he could. This was because as people generally do not want to believe in the unpleasant consequences which their own mistakes and obstinacy have brought upon them.

Meanwhile, the good Earl of Kent, who, though banished by Lear, and would lose his life if he were found in Britain, chose to stay and bear all consequences as long as there was a chance of his being useful to the king, his master. It is destiny sometimes that makes one submit to such mean circumstances. The Earl of Kent remained in the disguise of a serving-man with all his greatness and pomp laid aside. This good Earl offered his services to the king. The king not knowing him to be Kent in that disguise was pleased with the plainness, or rather bluntness, of his answers, which the Earl put on as the king was tired of the smooth, oily flattery which had no relation with reality. A bargain was quickly made, and Lear took Kent into his service by the name of Caius, never suspecting him to be his once great favourite,

Glossary
Bluntness strongly forthright

the high and mighty Earl of Kent.

Time passed by. Caius quickly found a way to show his fidelity and love to his royal master. It so happened that Goneril's steward misbehaved with Lear by giving him saucy looks and using foul language for which he was secretly encouraged by His mistress. Caius, could not bear to see His Majesty be insulted thus. And so he tripped up his heels and laid this unmannerly slave in the kennel. Seeing this friendly attitude, Lear became more and more attached to him.

Now Kent was not the only friend Lear had. In his respect, there was a fool, the court jester who was in his palace also and who used to entertain the king after he sorted serious matters. This was the fashion of the day to keep fools who would amuse the king. This poor fool clung to Lear after he had given away his crown, and by his witty sayings would keep up his good-humour. But many a time he would make fun of him for his imprudence in uncrowning himself and giving all away to his daughters.

Glossary
Unmannerly not having or exhibiting good manners

And in such wild sayings, and scraps of songs, of which he had plenty, this pleasant, honest fool poured out his heart even when Goneril herself was present!

Lear had begun to observe his daughter's lack of respect for him. She now plainly told him that his staying in her palace was inconvenient and more so due to the hundred knights.

She also added, 'Father, this expense of keeping these knights is useless and only serves to fill my court with confusion and feasting.'

She requested him to lessen their number and keep none but old men about him, such as himself.

Lear at first could not believe that it was his daughter who spoke so unkindly to him. He could not believe that she who had received a crown from him could ask him to cut off his train of knights and deprive him the respect due to his old age.

But when Gonoril persisted in her unlawful demand, the old man flew into a rage as the

Glossary
Inconvenient not comfortable, difficult

hundred knights were all men of high ranks having sobriety of manners and were all skilled. He was so angry that he called her a 'detested kite' and said that she did not speak the truth. They were not given to disorderly behaviour or feasting, as Gonoril had said. And he ordered his horses to be prepared, for he would go to his other daughter, Regan.

He cursed his eldest daughter, Goneril, and said, 'May God never bless her with a child, or, if she had, may it live to return that scorn and contempt which she had shown to me! May she feel how sharper than a serpent's tooth it was to have a thankless child.'

And Goneril's husband, the Duke of Albany hearing this, began making excuses in fear that Lear might think him to be unkind but Lear would not hear him at all! In a terrible fit of rage he ordered his horses to be saddled and set out with his followers for the abode of Regan, his other daughter. And Lear thought to himself, 'How could I punish Cordelia for speaking the truth.' He wept silently and then

Glossary
Sobriety to be sober

he was ashamed that such a creature as Goneril should have so much power over his manhood as to make him weep.

Meanwhile, Regan and her husband were redecorating their court in great pomp and show at their palace. Lear before reaching, send his servant Caius with letters to his daughter, so that she might be prepared for his reception, while he and his train followed after. But it seems that Goneril had been quicker in sending letters also to Regan accusing her father of waywardness and irritability, and advising her not to receive such a great train of knights as he was bringing with him. This messenger arrived at the same time with Caius, and when Caius met him he saw that it was the same old enemy the steward, whom he had formerly tripped up by the heels for his impudent behaviour to Lear. Caius not liking the fellow's look, and suspecting what he came for, began to abuse him and challenged him to fight, which the fellow refused. Caius, in a fit of honest passion, beat him soundly.

Glossary
Impudent rude; not having good manners

When Regan and her husband heard this; they ordered Caius to be put in the stocks, though he was a messenger from the king. The stock, Cains was in, was placed near the front door. This was done so that the first thing the king saw when he entered the castle was his faithful servant Caius sitting in that disgraceful situation.

Now, this was considered to be a bad omen of the reception which he could expect; but the worse was yet to come. The worst happened when, the king asked for his daughter and her husband, and he was told that they were weary with travelling all night and could not see him! And when, lastly, upon his insisting when they came to greet him, he saw the much hated Goneril, who had come to tell her own story and set her sister against the king her father already!

This sight was enough for the old man to be speechless in shock, and he was still more shattered to see Regan take Gonoril by the hand! Regan advised him to go home again

Glossary
Disgraceful shameful

with Goneril, and live with her peaceably. She said, 'Father, I think you should go back with Gonoril.'

She also dismissed half of his attendants, and

said that he should ask her forgiveness; for he was old and lacked foresight, and must be ruled and led by persons who have more judgement than him.

At this, Lear said that it would sound absurd if he were to go down on his knees and beg of his own daughter for food and other things! In a condition of great agitation he said, 'I will never return to Goneril and go for such an unnatural dependence! I will stay with you Regan with my train. Do not forget that I have given you half of my kingdom. I will stay with you as your eyes are not fierce as Goneril's but they are mild and kind. Instead of going back to Goneril, I would rather go over to France and beg a wretched pension from the king there, who has married my youngest daughter without a portion!'

Glossary
Agitation a condition of anxiety or excitement
Pension a payment received on the completion of a term of service

But he was mistaken in expecting kinder treatment from Regan than he had experienced from her sister Goneril. It was as if she was ready to outdo her sister in disrespectful behaviour. She declared that she thought fifty knights were too many for the old king; twenty five were enough. Then Lear, completely heartbroken, turned to Goneril and said that he would go back with her. But Goneril excused herself, and said, what is the need of so many as twenty five or even fifteen, when he might be waited upon by her servants or her sister's servants?

In this manner, these two wicked daughters treated their father as if struggling to exceed each other in cruelty to their old father, who had been so good to them. Little by little they would have lessened him of all his train and all respect.

Not that a splendid train is essential to happiness, but from being a king to a beggar is a hard change; from commanding millions to be without one attendant seemed to be very unacceptable. But it was ingratitude of his daughters that pierced this poor king's heart. He was also mentally vexed to think for having so foolishly given away a kingdom. His intellect began to be unsettled. But even in such a state of turmoil he vowed revenge against those unnatural hags.

While King Lear was thus idly threatening what his weak arm could never execute, night fell and with it came a loud storm of thunder and lightning with rain. As his daughters were not ready to admit his followers, he called for his horses, and chose rather to face the utmost fury of the storm outside than to stay under the same roof with his ungrateful daughters. And the daughters said that men who bring sufferings upon themselves should be punished thus. So, they shut the doors upon him!

The winds were strong, and the rain and the storm increased. The old king struggled to survive within these natural adversities which according to him were less sharp than his

Glossary
Adversities misfortunes and troubles

daughters' unkindness. For many miles there wasn't a bush or a tree; and the king stood in the open meadow exposed to the fury of the storm in the dark night.

The old king blinded by grief and betrayal said, 'May this storm blow the earth into the sea so that no ungrateful animal as man may survive!'

The old king was now left with the poor fool, who still abided with him, with his merry jokes trying to overcome their misfortune.

This great monarch also found his ever-faithful servant the good Earl of Kent, now transformed to Caius, with him. Caius who always followed close at his side, though the king did not know him to be the earl said, 'Alas, sir, why are you here? Creatures who love night will not love nights as these. This dreadful storm has driven the beasts to their hiding-places. Man's nature cannot endure so much suffering or fear.'

And Lear rebuked him and said, 'These evils are nothing in comparison to the greater miseries which exist.'

Glossary
Rebuked to express sharp disapproval or criticism of (someone) because of their behaviour or actions

But even after listening to the old king's lamentations the good Caius still persisted in his entreaties. He said that the king should not stay out in the open air amidst all the turmoil nature was offering. He at last persuaded him to enter a little wretched hut which stood upon the meadow. The fool first entered it and, suddenly ran back terrified, saying that he had seen a spirit. But when they examined the inside of the hut it was found that this spirit proved to be nothing more than a poor Bedlam beggar who had crept into this deserted hut for shelter.

Seeing the poor beggar the old king gave a long, wild speech. And from this and many such wild speeches which he uttered the good Caius understood that the king was not in the right frame of mind, and that his daughters' selfish behaviour had really made him go mad! And now the loyalty of this worthy Earl of Kent found opportunity to show his loyalty to the old king, his master even more.

Glossary
Wretched to be in a very unhappy and miserable state

With the assistance of some of the king's attendants who remained loyal, Caius' removed Lear at daybreak to the castle of Dover, where his own friends chiefly existed. But the Earl himself hastened to France, to the court of Cordelia, and described the terrible condition of her royal father telling her all about her sisters' cruelties.

Hearing all this, the good and loving child with many tears pleaded the king, her husband to give her permission to set out for England, with a sufficient powerful army to subdue her cruel sisters and their husbands and restore her father to his throne. Her wish was at once granted and she set forth with a royal army and landed at Dover.

Meanwhile, seeing the pitiable condition of the old king, the Earl of Kent had appointed some guardians to look after him. But unfortunately, Lear, having by some chance escaped from these guardians and was found by some of Cordelia's train, wandering about the fields near Dover. He was in a miserable condition, stark mad, and singing aloud to himself, with a crown upon his head which he had made of straw and wild weeds. Cordelia desperately wanted to meet her poor father. But the physicians advised her to put off this meeting till he gained his composure through sleep and treatment which was done using herbs.

With the aid of these skilful physicians, to whom Cordelia promised all her gold and jewels for the recovery of the old king, Lear was soon in a condition to see his daughter.

It was a tender sight to see the meeting between this father and daughter.

'O father, why did you misunderstand me? My love for you is much more than you will ever know!' said Cordelia, weeping.

At this, the poor old king held her hand and said, 'Forgive me dear child. Though I love you the most, I could not understand your simple but true words!'

The poor old king was ashamed at receiving

Glossary
Composure calmness of manner

such filial kindness from her whom he had cast off for so small a fault. Both these passions struggling with the remains of his disease, made him forget where he was or who was speaking to him so kindly. And then, he begged the people who stood by not to laugh at him if he were mistaken in thinking this lady to be his daughter Cordelia! Not only this, he also fell on his knees to beg pardon from his child. Seeing this, Cordelia was in much pain.

She would kneel and say, 'Father, it is my duty to kneel before you as I am your child, your Cordelia. Bless me father!'

Saying this, she kissed him and said that she was kissing away all her sisters' unkindness, and said that they might be ashamed of themselves, to turn their old kind father out into the cold air. She also told her father how she had come from France with the purpose to bring him assistance.

'I have come here to assist you father in getting back your throne,' said Cordelia.

'Dear Cordelia, you must forget and forgive your old father for I did not realize what I was doing! I am old and foolish,' said the old king.

So we will leave this old king in the protection of his dutiful and loving daughter, where, by the help of sleep and medicine, she and her physicians at length succeeded in curing his restless mind which was caused by the cruelty of his other daughters.

Meanwhile, an elderly nobleman the Earl of Gloucester was also experiencing family problems. His illegitimate son, Edmund, tricked him into believing that his own lawful son, Edgar, was trying to kill him. Edgar after escaping the manhunt that his father has set for him, disguises himself as a crazy beggar and calls himself 'Poor Tom'. Like Lear, he too heads out into the meadows.

When the loyal Gloucester realizes that Lear's daughters have turned against their father, he decides to help Lear in spite of the danger. Regan and her husband, Cornwall, discover him helping Lear, accuse him of treason, blind him, and turn him out to wander the countryside. But fortunately he ends up being led by his own disguised son, Edgar, towards the city of Dover, where Lear had also been brought.

Meanwhile, the ungrateful daughters of King Lear could not be faithful to their own husbands. Both Goneril and Regan soon grew tired of showing duty and affection to their husbands. Very soon, they began to show their affection for another man openly. Ironically, the object of their guilty love was the same. It was Edmund, the illegitimate son of the late Earl of Gloucester, who by his treacheries had

Glossary
Disguised to give a different appearance in order to hide one's original identity

succeeded in disinheriting his brother Edgar, the lawful heir, from his earldom, and by his wicked practices was now earl himself. Edmund was an intensely wicked man, and a fit object for the love of such wicked creatures as Goneril and Regan.

At that time the Duke of Cornwall, Regan's husband, dies and Regan immediately declares her intention of marrying this new Earl of Gloucester. Now this creates a lot of jealousy in her sister, to whom this wicked earl had at sundry times professed love. Goneril decides to end Regan's life which she did with poison. But soon she is imprisoned by her husband, the Duke of Albany, for this deed, and for her unlawful love for the earl which he had heard about. Goneril in a fit of disappointed love and rage shortly puts an end to her own life. Thus the justice of Heaven at last overtakes these wicked daughters.

While the eyes of all men were upon this event, admiring the justice displayed in their deserved deaths, the same eyes were suddenly shocked

Glossary
Disinheriting to take steps to prevent someone from inheriting one's property
Imprisoned kept in prison in a captive state

to see how this same power brought misfortune on the young and virtuous daughter, the Lady Cordelia, whose good deeds deserved a more fortunate conclusion. But it is an awful truth that innocence and goodness are not always successful in this world. The armed forces which Goneril and Regan had sent out under the command of the new Earl of Gloucester were victorious, and Cordelia was taken a prisoner. She ended her life in prison. Thus heaven took away this innocent lady to itself in her young years, after showing the world a matchless example of a child's duty. Lear also met his death soonafter.

Before he died, the good Earl of Kent,

who had still attended his old master's steps tried to make him understand that it was he who had followed him under the name of Caius; but Lear did not understand due to his insanity the simple fact that Kent and Caius was the same person. So Kent thought it futile to trouble him with explanations at such a time. After Lear passed away, very soon this follower of the king too followed him to the grave due to grief and old age.

How the bad Earl of Gloucester, whose treasons were discovered, and was killed by his brother, the lawful earl, is another story. How Goneril's husband, the Duke of Albany, who was not at all responsible for the death of Cordelia, and had never encouraged his lady in her wicked proceedings against her father, ascended the throne of Britain is yet another tale to tell.

Glossary
Futile ineffective

Post-reading Activities

1. Name the three daughters of King Lear.
2. Write a short note on Lear's youngest daughter Cordelia.
3. What is the role of Earl of Kent in the play?
4. Enumerate the sufferings of King Lear which ultimately drove him insane.
5. Make a character analysis of King Lear.
6. Who had accompanied Lear when he left Regan's house? What is the significance of this character?
7. Discuss the importance of the subplot involving the Earl of Gloucester and his two sons.
8. Who was Caius? What kind of a person do you think he was?
9. Do you think Shakespeare has done justice to the ending to the play?
10. Suggest an alternative ending of the play.

About the Author

William Shakespeare was an English poet and playwright, universally acknowledged to be the greatest writer in English language. He is considered to be the world's pre-eminent dramatist also. He lived in the age of Queen Elizabeth I when England enjoyed a time of immense prosperity and stability. He is often called England's national poet and the 'Bard of Avon'.

It is indeed strange that though Shakespeare is recognized as one of literature's greatest influences, very little is actually known about him. Whatever we know about his life comes from the registrar records, court records, wills, marriage certificates and his tombstone.

Glossary

Playwright a person who composes plays

Early Life

William Shakespeare was born in Stratford-on-Avon, the son of John Shakespeare, a glove maker and dealer in wool. John was a prominent man in Stratford. William's mother was Mary Arden who was the youngest daughter in her family. She inherited much of her father's landowning and farming estate when he died. William was the third child of John and Mary Shakespeare.

Shakespeare probably attended Stratford Grammar School in his childhood. When he was 18, he married Anne Hathaway in 1582. At that time Anne was 26, and already three months pregnant. After sometime his daughter, Susanna, was born. It is generally thought that he must have been in Stratford when Hamnet and Judith, his other two children were born in 1585.

Between the years 1580s and 1592, what Shakespeare did is unknown because no records of his life and works exist of that period. This period of time is often referred to as the 'lost years'. It is possible that he spent this entire period in London after leaving Stratford to escape a charge of deer poaching. Some records say that he was employed at a playhouse 'in a very mean Rank' during this time. Researchers make assumptions that during these 'lost years', Shakespeare might have tended horses for theatergoers or worked as a sailor, a teacher or a coachman.

Some think that he might have been a soldier, a law clerk, a theater page, or a moneylender. He could have held several of these jobs or he may have held none of them!

Shakespeare may also have spent the time travelling to far off towns or even to foreign countries. His plays suggest that he visited Italy, for more than a dozen of them including *The Merchant of Venice, Romeo and Juliet, All's Well That Ends Well, Othello, Coriolanus, Julius Caesar, The Two Gentlemen of Verona, The Taming of the Shrew, Titus Andronicus, Much Ado About Nothing*, and *The Winter's Tale*, all have scenes set in Italy.

Career

How Shakespeare first started his career in the theatre no one knows for certain. Whether an acting troupe recruited Shakespeare in his hometown or he was forced on his own to travel to London to begin his career, is not clearly known. In the year 1592 came the first reference to Shakespeare in the world of theatre when Robert Greene an eminent writer of that time mentioned him in his writing. While in London, Shakespeare lived alone in rented accommodations while his wife and children remained in Stratford. Why his family did not move to London with him is unknown.

In 1592, when an epidemic of plague closed the theatres,

the versatile Shakespeare wrote sonnets and other poetry until the theatres reopened in 1594. The same year, he joined a newly formed drama group called the 'Lord Chamberlain's Men', serving there as a writer and an actor.

Shakespeare produced most of his well-known works between 1589 and 1613. His early plays were mainly comedies and histories, the literary genre which he raised to the peak of artistic sophistication by the end of the 16th century. He then wrote mainly tragedies until about 1608, including *Hamlet*, *King Lear*, *Othello*, and *Macbeth*, all of which are considered to be the finest works in the English language. In the last years of his career, he wrote tragicomedies, also known as romances, and collaborated with other playwrights.

Shakespeare's works are the greatest representation of art from Elizabethan England. They encompass the economic, social, and educational aspects of life in a nice, neat package. No other art form, including painting, could provide so much information about life in Elizabethan England.

Theatre in Shakespeare's Times

During the age of Shakespeare, all plays which were written

Glossary
Versatile able to adapt to many different functions or activities

had to be approved by the government's censor. This is because plays at that time were considered morally or politically offensive and could be banned. It was considered so very offensive that many a time the playwright would be imprisoned too.

Shakespeare presented his plays at inns, courtyards, royal palaces, private residences, playhouses and the Globe Theatre built in 1599. The playhouses in Shakespeare's time were wooden structures with tiers of seating galleries in the shape of a horseshoe. They could seat two thousand to three thousand people who paid two or more pennies. It is believed that at that time the theatre lovers who were wealthy could pay extra to sit on the stage! The main floor, which was surrounded by the galleries, had no roof and no seats. A person could stand and watch the play standing by paying a penny. This area was called a 'pit'. Up to one thousand people could stand and watch performances in this area under a hot sun or dark clouds.

The stage of the Globe theatre was four to six feet above ground level. There was no curtain that opened or closed at the beginning or at the end of the plays. A wall with two or three doors leading to the dressing rooms of the actors stood at the back of the stage. These rooms collectively were known as the 'tiring house'.

Males played all the characters, even that of women! Actors

Glossary
Imprisoned kept in prison in a captive state

played gods, ghosts, demons, and other supernatural characters. They could pop up from the underworld through a trap door on the stage or descend down to Earth from heaven on a winch line from the ceiling. The sound of thunder was created off stage, by beating a sheet metal. To demonstrate that an actor had suffered a fencing wound, he simply had to slap his hand against a pouch beneath his shirt to release 'blood' showing his death.

Globe Theatre

Although Shakespeare's plays were performed at different venues during the playwright's career, the Globe Theatre in the Southwark district of London was the place at which his best known plays were first performed. The Globe was built during Shakespeare's early period in 1599 by one of his long-standing associates, Cuthbert Burbage.

The theater that Cuthbert Burbage built had a total capacity between 2,000 and 3,000 spectators. Due to the absence of electric lights, all performances at the Globe were conducted during the day (probably in the mid-afternoon spanning between 2 p.m. and 5 p.m.). As most of the stage of the Globe Theatre was open air and the apparatus for sound system were poor, the actors were compelled to shout their lines, stress their intonations, and engage themselves in exaggerated theatrical gestures.

Glossary
Spectator a person who watches something—a show, a game, or any other event
Apparatus the equipment or machinery needed for a particular activity

The plays which were staged at the Globe were completely devoid of background scenery although costumes and props were utilized. There was no proscenium arch, no curtains, and no stagehands than the actors themselves. Instead, changes of scenes were suggested in the speeches and narrative situations of the plays.

End of Globe Theatre

The original structure of the Globe Theatre existed until June 29, 1613, when its thatched roof was set on fire by a cannon fired during the performance of the play Henry VIII. The Globe burned to ashes and could not be saved. At this time, Shakespeare had almost retired and was at Stratford-on-Avon where he died three years later at the age of fifty-two. The Globe was reconstructed in the year 1614.

Glossary
Proscenium arch it is a kind of an arch which forms a framing on the opening between the stage and the auditorium in some theatres